Theorem Appliqué: Book 1

ABUNDANT HARVEST

by Patricia B. Campbell and Mimi Ayars

Chitra Publications
2 Public Avenue
Montrose, Pennsylvania 18801

First printing: 1994

Campbell, Patricia B. (Patricia Bojan)
Theorem appliqué / by Patricia B. Campbell and Mimi Ayars.
p. cm.
Contents: Bk. 1. Abundant harvest
ISBN 0-9622565-9-5 (v. 1)
1. Appliqué--Patterns. 2. Wall hangings. I. Ayars, Mimi.
II. Title. III. Title: Abundant harvest.
TT779.C367 1994
746.44'50433--dc20 94-31563
CIP

Editor: Janice P. Johnson
Design and Illustration: Kimberly L. Grace
Front cover and color photography: Guy Cali Associates, Clarks Summit, PA
Back cover quilt: Stephen J. Appel Photography, Vestal, NY
Black and white photography: Bradley Chrisenberry, Dallas, TX

Dedicated to
Pat's brother, Douglas H. Bojan, her biggest fan
and Mimi's quiltmaking sisters, her best supporters

In Appreciation
We would like to thank the following people for their contributions to "Abundant Harvest."

Jeffrey Gutcheon, The American Classic Line	Background fabric
Elliott Morgan, Morgan & Associates	Quilting stand
H. D. Wilbanks, Jr., Hobbs Bonded Fibers	Wool batting
Sally Ashbacher	Stitcher and Embroiderer
Sharon Chambers	Stitcher and Quiltmaker (back cover)
Sadako Cunningham	Stitcher
Michelle Jack	Quilter and Pattern Drafting
Jennifer Patriarche	Stitcher
Joanna Shampine	Stitcher

"Earth is here so kind, that just tickle her with a hoe and she laughs with a harvest."
—Douglas Jerrold

INTRODUCTION

A fad swept the U.S. during the middle 1900s. It was Paint by Number. Men, women and children bought kits that contained a canvas board with a printed picture divided into small areas, each marked with a number. There were also cups of oil paint of appropriate shades numbered to correspond to the numbered spaces, and a brush.

Many would-be artists filled in the spaces, making the finished product look like a coloring book rendition. Other aspiring artists showed talent in blending and the finished product was sufficiently passable to be framed and hung with pride to decorate a room. Today it is hard to find a sample of Paint by Number.

Another fad swept our country during the early 1800s. It was Theorem Painting. In many ways the two were similar, but theorem painting was done, as far as we know, only by girls and women.

Painting had overtaken embroidery as the test of femininity. Talented women painted free hand and those who were less than talented used stencils called "theorems." An artist designed a picture for which a series of stencils was cut, either by the professional or the would-be painter. Unlike the single stencil that leaves unpainted areas among the shapes, a series of stencils, used in order, resulted in a composition that looked very much like a traditional painting. They were not done on canvas, but on paper, silk and velvet. The most popular was velvet. Although these pictures graced many a home, few have survived. Some prime examples that did survive can be seen at the Abby Aldrich Rockefeller Folk Art Center in Williamsburg, Virginia, the Smithsonian Institute in Washington D. C., Old Sturbridge Village in Sturbridge, Massachusetts, and the Shelburne Museum in Shelburne,Vermont. Recently there has been a revival of theorem painting on velvet with "authentic" reproductions done by recognized craft persons.

In the spirit of this antique art form, Patricia B. Campbell has created theorem appliqué designs for "Abundant Harvest," a 42" x 42" wall hanging. Mimi Ayars has written concise instructions with illustrations to guide stitchers of all levels.

This book contains all the necessary information for making a wall hanging that will reflect the theorem paintings of old. Three more books will follow, all theorem appliqué. The wall hangings, designed around different themes, will be kept secret until they are published. Each will be a little more challenging than the one before, with the last one being a burst of glory and a showpiece of skill.

PREPARATION

MATERIALS

- 2 yards of 45" background fabric. Use off-white to mimic the velvet of old theorem paintings. Choose high quality 100% cotton that is woven on grain so that the finished work hangs well. Gutcheon's The American Classic Line™ was used in "Abundant Harvest."
- For the design pieces, go through your scrap bag, trade swatches with friends, and buy fat eighths and fat quarters from shops. Cotton eases needle-turning, which makes your stitches beautiful. A wide palette of shades and prints allows you to reproduce realistic fruits and vegetables. Use your imagination when choosing colors or use the photos of the wall hanging as a guide.
- 1/2 yard brown for the binding. Choose one of the brown fabrics you are using in the blocks and border.
- 1 1/2 yards of 45" backing fabric.
- 1 1/4 yards of 45" lightweight batting. The batt in "Abundant Harvest" is lightweight wool from Hobbs. It needles easily and hangs well.
- A variety of threads to match the appliqué fabrics. Mettler #60 and DMC® #50 machine embroidery thread were used in "Abundant Harvest" because they blend well with fabrics for stitches that are nearly invisible.
- Dark olive green and black-brown embroidery floss for the tendrils and stems.
- Off-white quilting thread.
- Package of inexpensive lightweight, non-fusible, non-woven interfacing (3 yards by 15") for the master patterns.
- Clear plastic template material. When you can see through the templates you have more freedom in fabric placement of the design pieces.

EQUIPMENT LIST

- Silver, white and mechanical lead pencils for marking. Do not use yellow, which contains wax. It can mar your work if touched by a hot iron.
- Permanent black marker for tracing master patterns. A Sharpie® ultra-fine point permanent marker is recommended.
- Sharp scissors for fabric and craft scissors for cutting template plastic.
- Sharp pins—sashiko, sequin and quilting.
- Pincushion.
- Sandpaper board to keep fabric from slipping when drawing around templates.
- Needles (#10 and #12 betweens) for appliqué and for quilting. A small needle is recommended for both processes.
- Thimble. Those tiny needles can pierce a finger!
- Good light. You must see well to stitch well.
- Comfortable chair to avoid fatigue.
- Ruler for marking blocks and borders.
- Sewing machine for assembling the quilt top.
- Rotary cutter and mat. These are not essential, but they are nice for cutting blocks and border strips.

CUTTING BLOCKS, BORDERS & BINDING

Wash the fabric or don't, as you prefer. Do not bother to cut away the selvage; it will be removed later. Refer to the illustration below for cutting guide. Cut the lengthwise pieces before the cross-wise. Be sure to cut the pieces square and on grain.

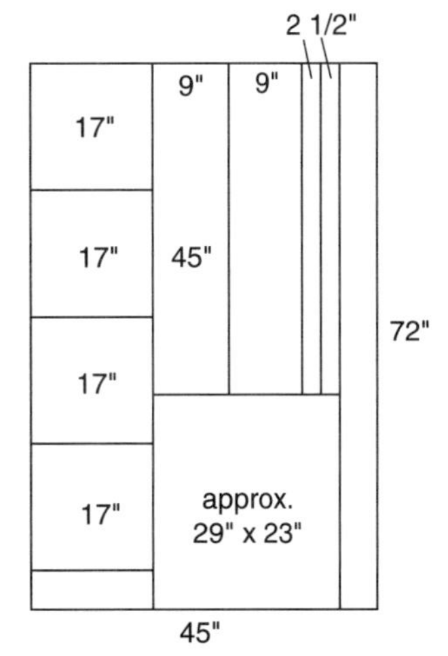

As soon as each piece is cut, tag the right side and top of the fabric with a small square of paper in the upper right corner. This is to insure that the pieces have the grain going in the same direction and that all are stitched on the right side. Note the position of the tags on the border pieces.

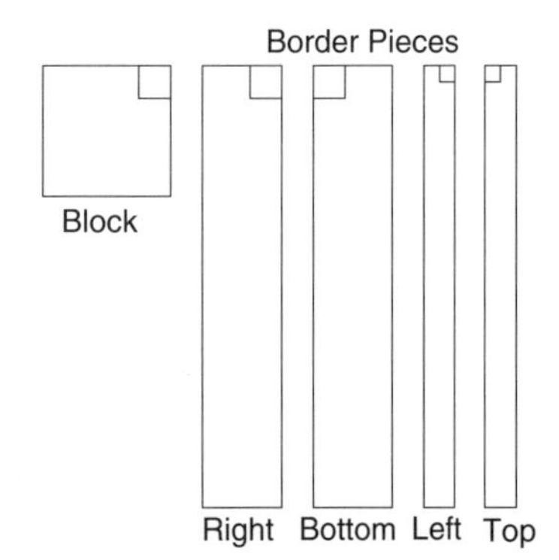

Cut from the background fabric:

- Two border strips 9" x 45". These will finish to 8" x 42".
- Two border strips 2 1/2" x 45". These will finish to 2" x 42".
- Four 17" x 17" blocks. These will be finished to 16" x 16" when the quilt is assembled.

Cut from the brown binding fabric:

- Five 1 1/4" wide strips across the width of the fabric. You will need a total of 176". (If you prefer to use the same material as the background, there will be a long strip of leftover fabric after the blocks and border pieces have been cut. You can get three 1 1/4" x 72" pieces from this.) Cut the strips on the straight grain of the fabric and sew them right sides together, end to end, with 1/4" bias seams. Finger press the seams open without stretching.

MASTER PATTERNS

Cut from interfacing:

- Four 15" squares for the blocks.
- One 7 1/2" x 32" strip of interfacing for the right border.
- One 7 1/2" x 40" strip of interfacing for the bottom border.

Each block pattern is divided into four parts. Each part appears on a separate page. Trace the quadrants of the blocks onto the squares of interfacing with permanent black marker, matching up the broken lines and the center points of the pattern in the book.

The border pattern is shown in sections with a single section per page. Miter the corners of the wide strips of interfacing and trim the seam. First trace the corner section, making sure the miter of the interfacing follows the diagonal line in the book. Trace the remaining sections in numerical order, including the broken lines.

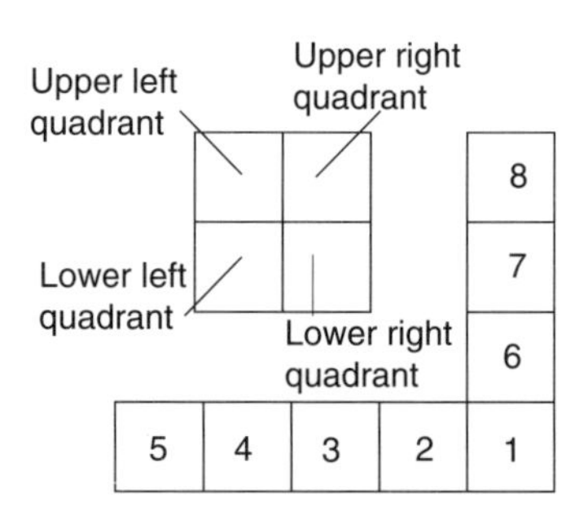

TRACING PATTERNS ON FABRIC

First, find the center of one 17" x 17" background fabric block by folding the square in half one way and then the other. Pinch where the folds come together. Open up and lightly mark with a pencil on the wrong side the point where the folds cross.

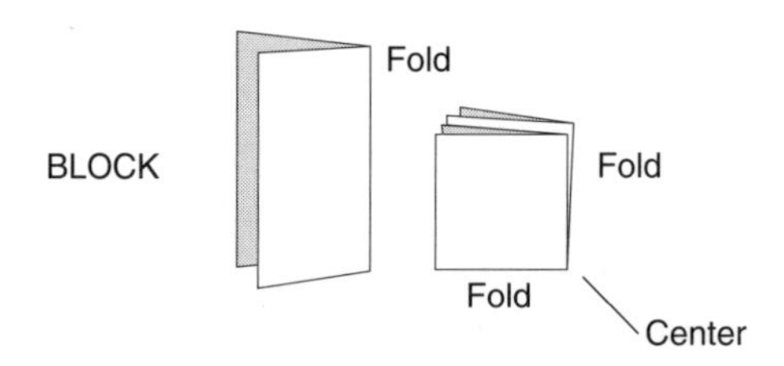

Lay your fabric right side up on top of an interfacing square that has been marked with the master pattern. Push a pin through the center of the right side of your block into the center of the interfacing pattern held beneath it. Square up the two.

Using a light box or placing white paper under the interfacing to see the lines more easily, mark the patterns on the right side of the fabric blocks. Keep your pencil lines 1/4" inside the master pattern marks so there is less chance of having to remove pencil lines when your stitching is completed. Use an 'x' for cherry and grape placement.

Miter the corner of the 9" x 45" background fabric border pieces. After sewing, trim the seam to 1/4" and finger press. Be careful not to stretch it.

To find the center of the bottom and right

border pieces, turn the fabric to the wrong side. Fold each piece lengthwise, right side to right side, and mark lightly along the fold.

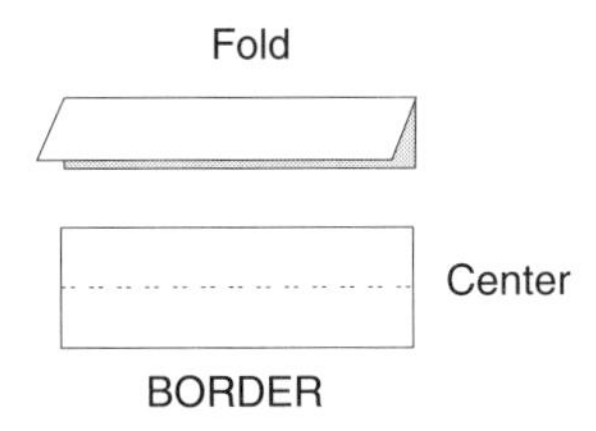

Align these marks with the broken lines on the master pattern. Be sure to match the diagonal line of the miter of the fabric and the diagonal line of the master pattern. Mark the pattern on the right side of the fabric, staying 1/4" inside the lines.

MAKING TEMPLATES

Using the Block 1 master pattern with white paper under it, draw templates of the various pieces on template material with a mechanical pencil. Cut out the templates carefully.

To make perfect circles for grapes, you must have perfectly round circle templates. Check to see if the templates have any little peaks. If so, smooth them with an emery board. After all the templates for the block have been cut, lay them in their proper place on the master pattern. Number the spaces on the master pattern and their corresponding templates with permanent black marker, if you wish.

MARKING AND CUTTING DESIGN PIECES

Pick up a template from the master pattern and lay it on the right side of your design fabric. To reduce fraying and ease needle-turning, place your templates on the bias grain of the fabric as often as possible. Trace around the template with a sharp pencil held so that the eraser end tips slightly outward, thus enabling you to get close to the template. A sandpaper board underneath the fabric helps keep the fabric from slipping. The marked line will be your stitching line. Cut out the pieces adding only a 1/8" seam allowance beyond the marked line. The slim seam allowance makes needle-turning much easier.

Pin the fabric pieces in place on the master pattern as you cut them. After all the pieces for Block 1 have been pinned, look at the arrangement to make sure you like what you see. If any piece "jumps out" or "dies," replace it. Do likewise for the other blocks and border. When all the pieces for "Abundant Harvest" have been pinned on the master patterns of the blocks and border, arrange them as they will be assembled and look again to see if you like the colors and fabric. When you're happy with the combination, you are ready to start stitching.

Store the templates for each block and border in separate labeled plastic bags.

STITCHING

Just as theorem painting was done in a specific order, theorem appliqué (like other appliqué designs) is done in a specific order. A series of stencils was essential to keep the paint of neighboring areas from running together. The artist painted the cutout spaces of Theorem Number 1 and let the paint dry before proceeding to the next theorem. In appliqué, the pieces are not only adjacent, but often overlapping. The appliqué artist can move from one part of the composition to another, just as the theorem artist did, as long as the bottom pieces are stitched first.

BASIC APPLIQUÉ

The narrow seam allowance on your design pieces makes clipping unnecessary. Knot a 15" to 18" piece of thread that matches the design fabric. Begin stitching on a gentle curve, never at a point. Bring the needle up from the back of the design fabric through the pencil line. With the tip about 3/4" from where the thread comes up, sweep the needle toward you, turning the seam allowance under.

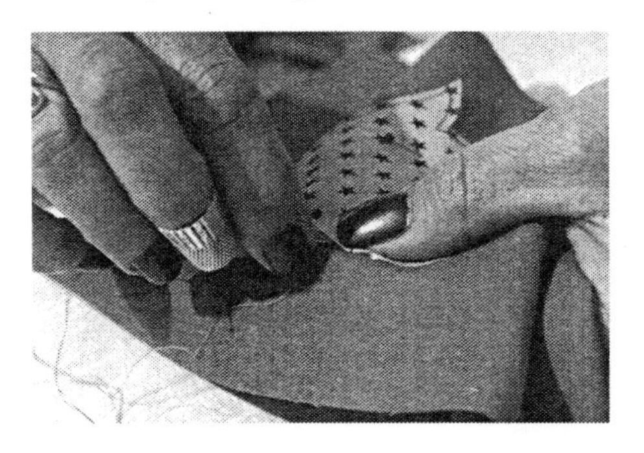

Put the needle point into the background fabric directly adjacent to where your thread emerged on the marked line and slightly under the fold of the design fabric. In one motion, pick up two or three threads of the background fabric and come up into the design fabric on the marked line (which is now the fold) about 1/16" from the last stitch.

Take several stitches and then needle-turn, sweeping the needle toward you. Continue in this manner. To minimize fatigue, make sure you position your hands so that your thumbs always face each other. When your thread is too short to continue, push the needle through to the back of the background fabric, just inside the edge of the design piece. Take a little "bite" of the background fabric with the needle as shown. Repeat with a second "bite."

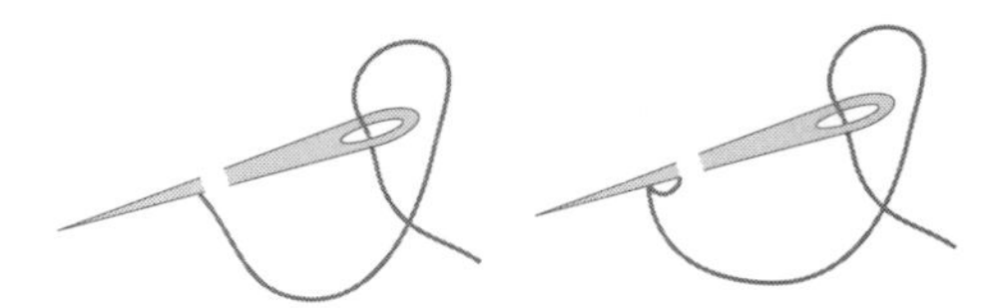

Bury the thread by passing the needle between the two layers, away from the edge. Snip the tail close to the background fabric. Re-thread the needle and make a knot. Bring the needle point up at the pencil line, very close to the last stitch. The new knot will be hidden in the fold. Proceed as before, stitching the piece in place

POINTS

Stitch up to the marked point. Take a second stitch on top of the last stitch to secure it. Remove your thimble and insert your threaded needle in the background fabric, out of the way. Turn the block as if you were going to start stitching down the other side of the piece. Clip off any little tail that sneaks out from the seam allowance of the first side.

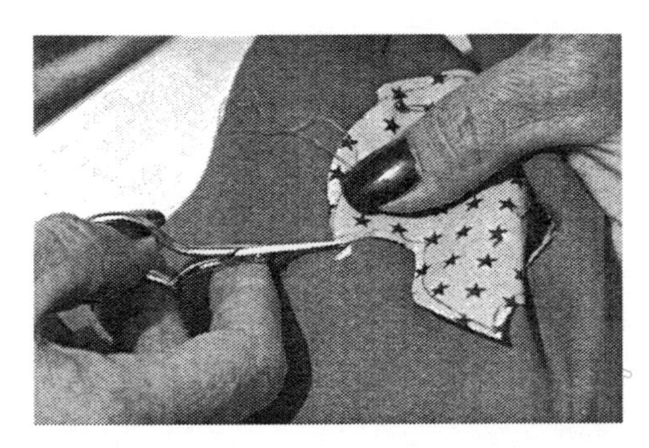

Hold the stitch at the point and the thread firmly under your thumbnail. With a quilter's pin grasped about 1/2" up from the point and braced from behind with your middle finger to strengthen it, sweep the seam allowance under from right to left, all the time holding the point tightly with your thumbnail, lifting it only when you sweep the fabric under. If you don't like the result, pull the seam allowance out with your needle and try again. Sweep right to left and then left to right.

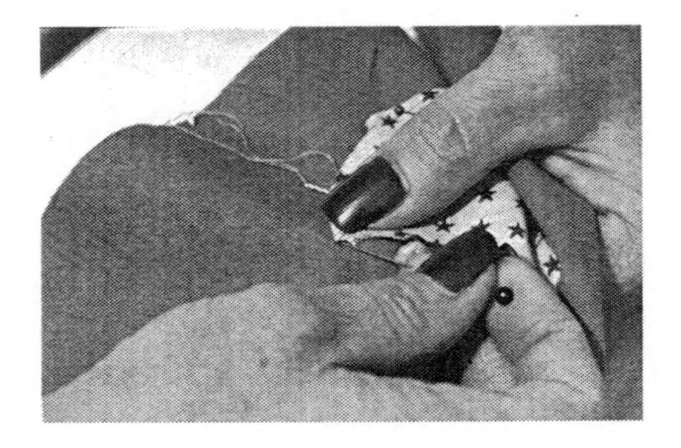

Still holding the point tightly with your thumbnail, take a 1/16" stitch out from the point into the background fabric. Unlike your other stitches which you've been trying to hide, you now want this one to show. The extra stitch elongates the point, giving the illusion that the tip is more pointed than it really is. Proceed stitching down the other side.

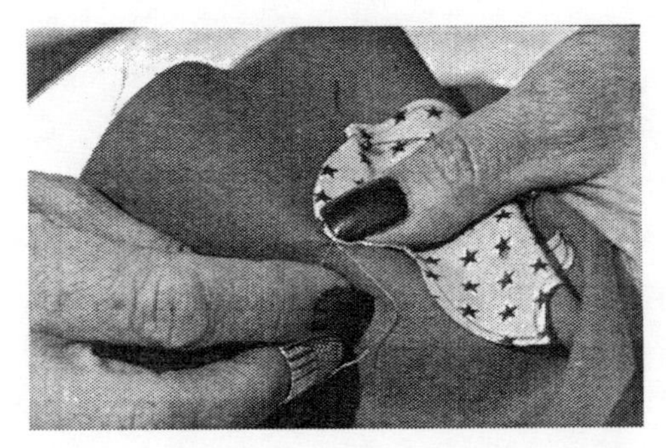

"V"

The "V" is the exception to the "don't clip the seam allowance" guideline. You'll need to clip in one place: *to* the marked line in the valley.

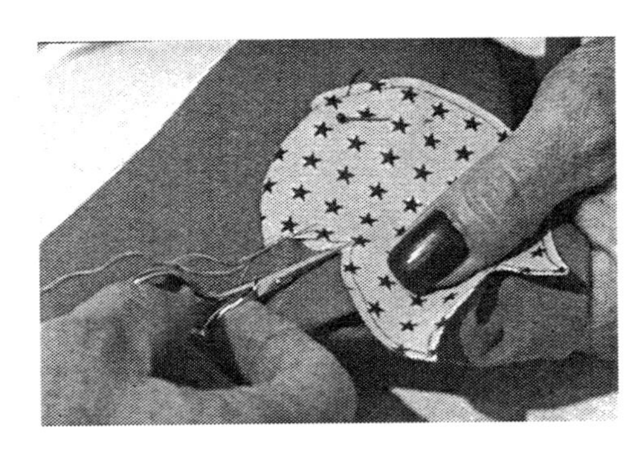

Start stitching above the valley and stitch to the clip. Flip under the unstitched side of the piece, creating a fold.

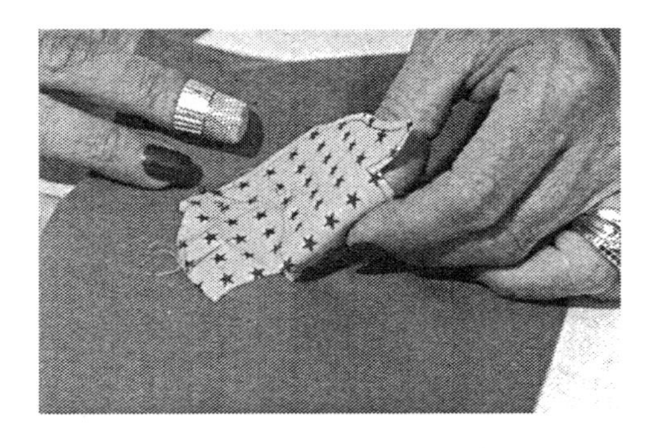

Take the next stitch. It should not be a bigger one or a smaller one—simply the next stitch.

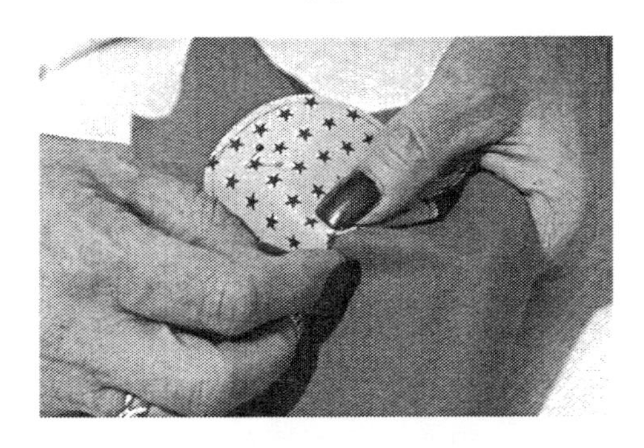

Slowly flip the unstitched fabric back in place.

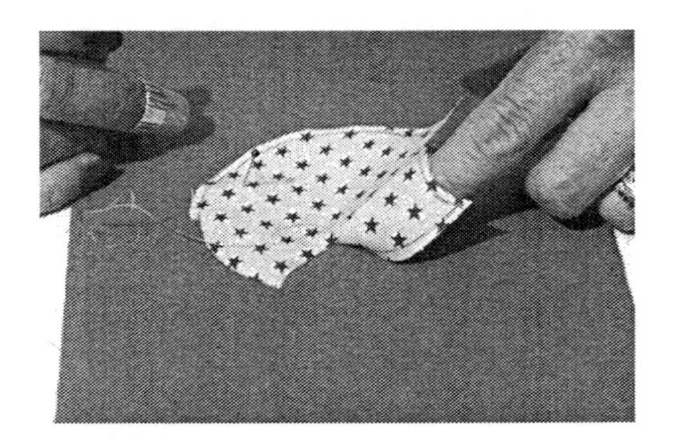

The seam allowance on the flipped part turns under and is now ready for you to continue stitching.

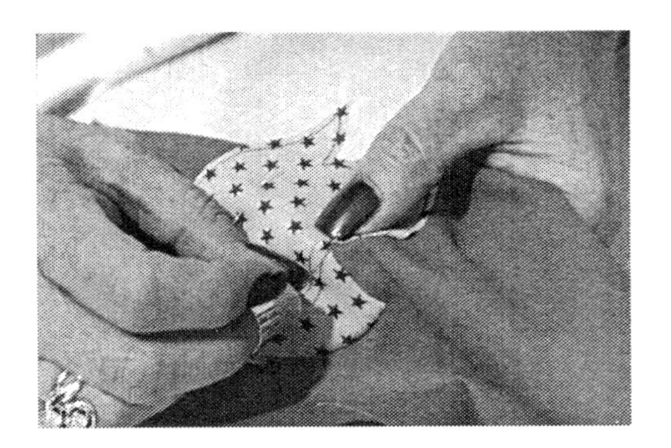

CIRCLES

You have made perfect circle templates and marked perfect circles on your design fabric. Now you are going to stitch perfect circles. There is no need to clip the seam allowance. Using a sequin pin on the underside to hold the circle in place, needle-turn only enough to take one stitch. Take that one stitch, turn the circle, needle-turn, then take another stitch. The steps of needle-turing, taking only one stitch, and turning the circle are what create a smooth circle.

EMBROIDERY

Theorem artists painted the tendrils and stems freehand after the stenciling was completed. To reflect this delicate painting, theorem appliquérs embroider the tendrils and stems after the appliqué is completed. Choose the stitch and colors you like. The back stitch was used in "Abundant Harvest" with dark olive green for the tendrils and black-brown for the stems.

FINISHING

Make a 16" x 16" cardboard template to help in block assembly. Find the center of the template by drawing diagonal lines from corner to corner. The center is the point where the lines intersect. Make a tiny hole at that point with the tip of your scissors. You have already made a light pencil mark on the back of your appliquéd block. With the appliquéd block face down, pass a pin through the hole of the cardboard template into the marked center of the block. Square the two. Mark with pencil all around the template. This will be your sewing line. Mark the other blocks in the same way. Sew the blocks in the positions illustrated. Trim the seams to 1/4" and press open or to one side, whichever you prefer.

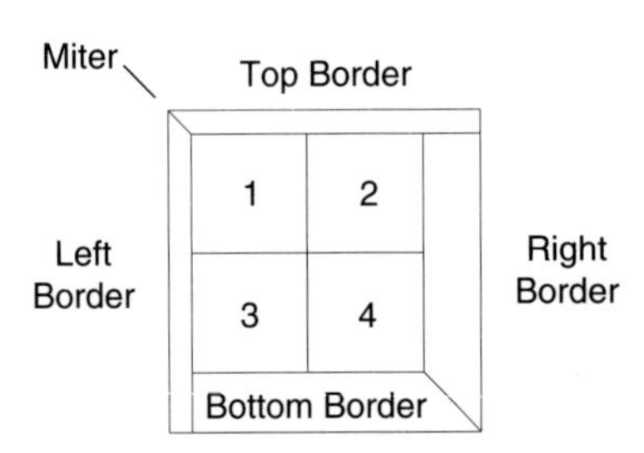

You have already made light pencil marks in the center of the wrong side of the bottom and right border pieces. Mark the stitching lines by measuring out 4" on each side of the marks and drawing lines. Sew the border to the assembled blocks along these lines. Do not worry about leftover fabric at the ends. Trim the seams to 1/4". Trim the remaining outside edge of the assembled blocks to 1/4".

Stitch the left and top borders together with a mitered corner. Trim the seam and finger press it open. With right sides together, match the raw edges of the border and the assembled blocks. Sew along the marked line of the blocks and straight across the ends of the bottom and right border pieces. Refer to the illustration above as necessary. Trim the seams to 1/4".

Press the top gently on the wrong side with a dry iron. Trim the outside edge of the bottom and right borders to a 1/4" seam allowance. They should now measure 8 1/4" wide. Do not trim the narrow border, which should measure 2 1/4" wide.

QUILTING

Cut the backing the full width of the fabric and 45" long. Baste the top, batt and backing together. Bring the extra backing fabric over to the front temporarily, basting with safety pins, to protect the edges while you quilt.

Make your own quilting design or use the design shown in the photo of "Abundant Harvest." Outline quilt the fruits and vegetables. Quilt diagonally in the background. When the quilting is finished, trim the backing and batting even with the front.

SLEEVE

No wall hanging is complete without a sleeve. It can be made from any fabric you like, but there is enough fabric allowed in the backing fabric requirement to make one.

Cut a 9" x 42" piece of fabric. Sew double 1/4" hems on the 9" sides. Measure down 1 1/2" from one of the 42" sides. Fold along this line, wrong sides together. Machine baste 1/2" in from the folded edge, forming a tuck in the sleeve. Fold the strip in half lengthwise, wrong sides together, with the raw edges of the 42" sides even. Making sure that the fold is facing out, pin, then sew the raw edges of the sleeve to the top edge of the quilt back with a 1/8" seam. Pin and tack the lower edge of the sleeve to the back of the wall hanging by hand. Be careful to stitch only through the backing fabric. Pull out the machine basting stitches.

SEWING ON THE BINDING

To keep the edges of the quilt straight, baste close to the edges before sewing on the binding. Start sewing the binding to the quilt, right sides together and raw edges even, about 2" away from one corner, leaving a 2" tail of binding free. Use any method for binding a quilt that you like, but be sure the corners are square. Stop sewing a few inches from where you began. Turn the first end back at a 45 degree angle and sew the last end straight down. Trim.

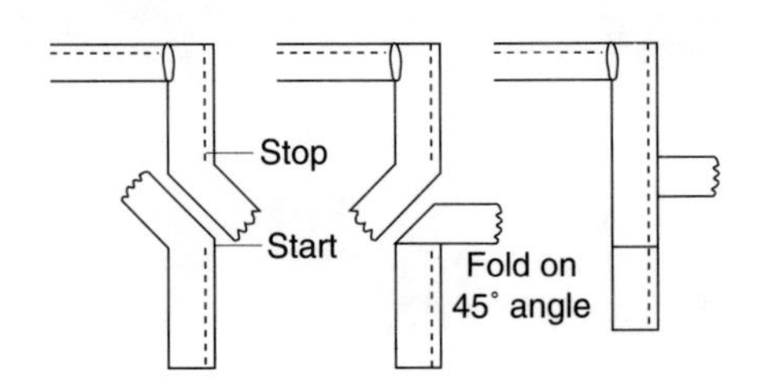

Turn the binding to the back, fold the raw edge under 1/4", pin, and stitch by hand. Tack the corners and the joining ends.

DOCUMENTATION

Make a label for your wall hanging, indicating the name "Abundant Harvest," (or a name of your choice), the date, your name, and any other important information you think your heirs might like to know. Sew the label onto the back. Hang the wall hanging in your home. Take a photo for your scrapbook. Show off your work of art.

Book II will follow soon. Look for it!

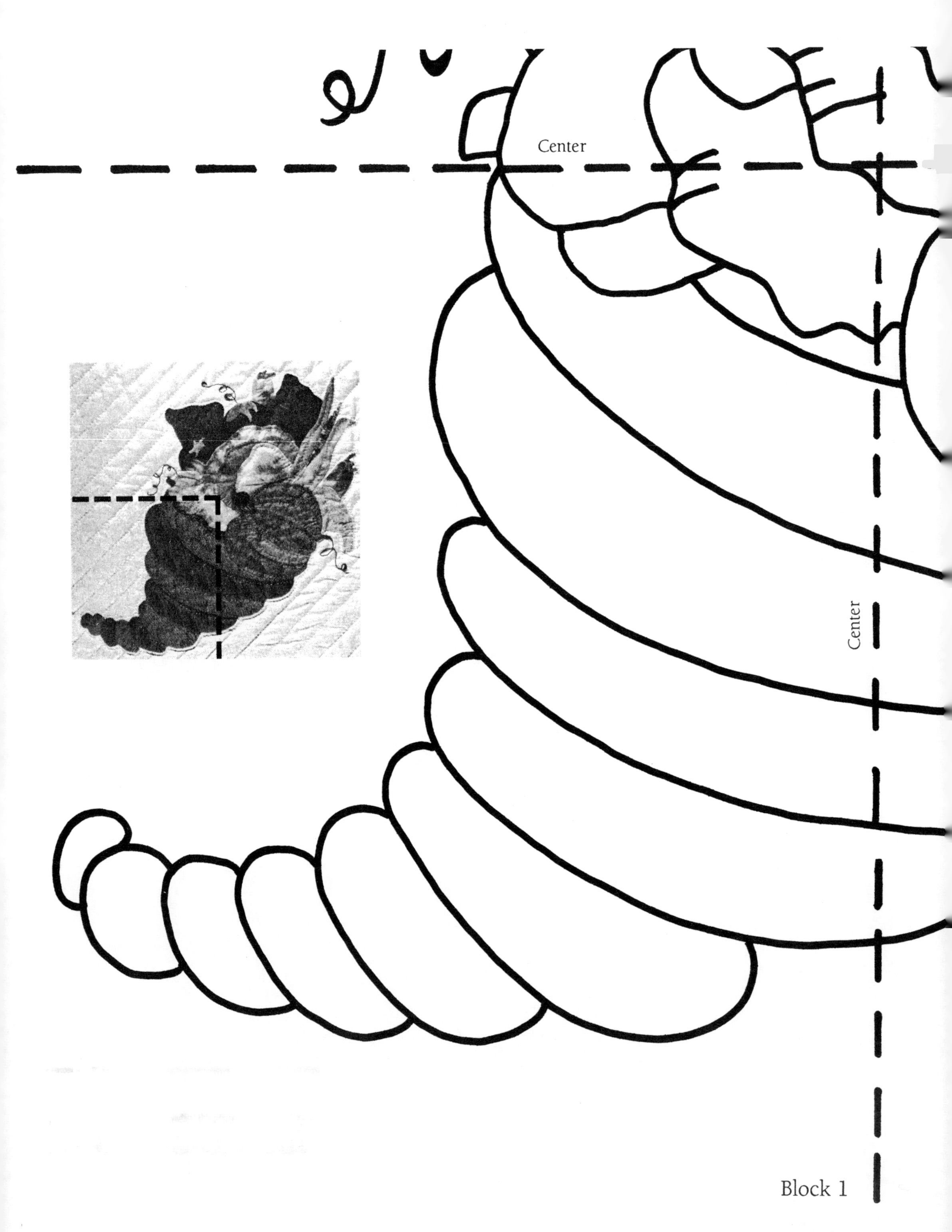
Center
Center
Block 1

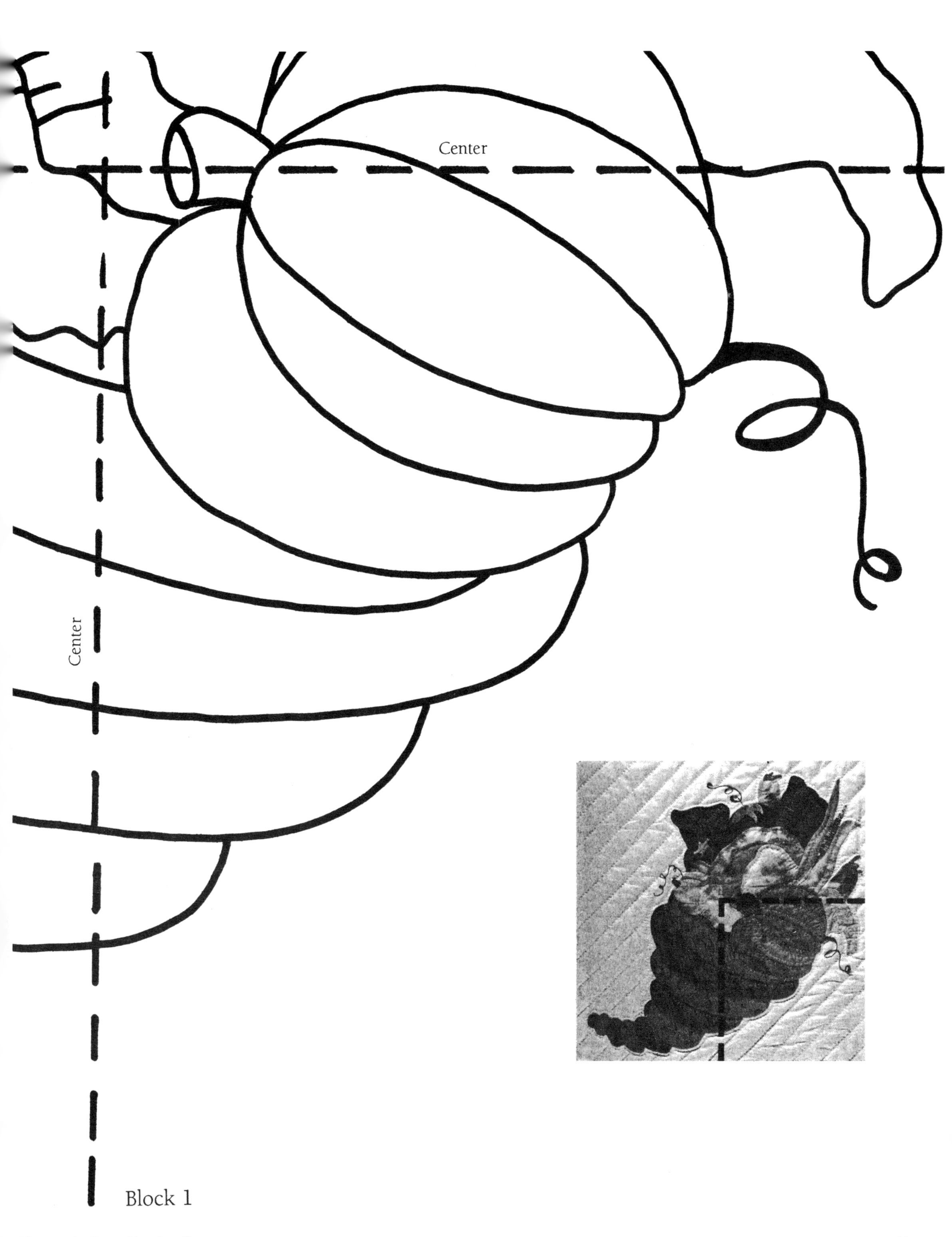
Center
Center
Block 1

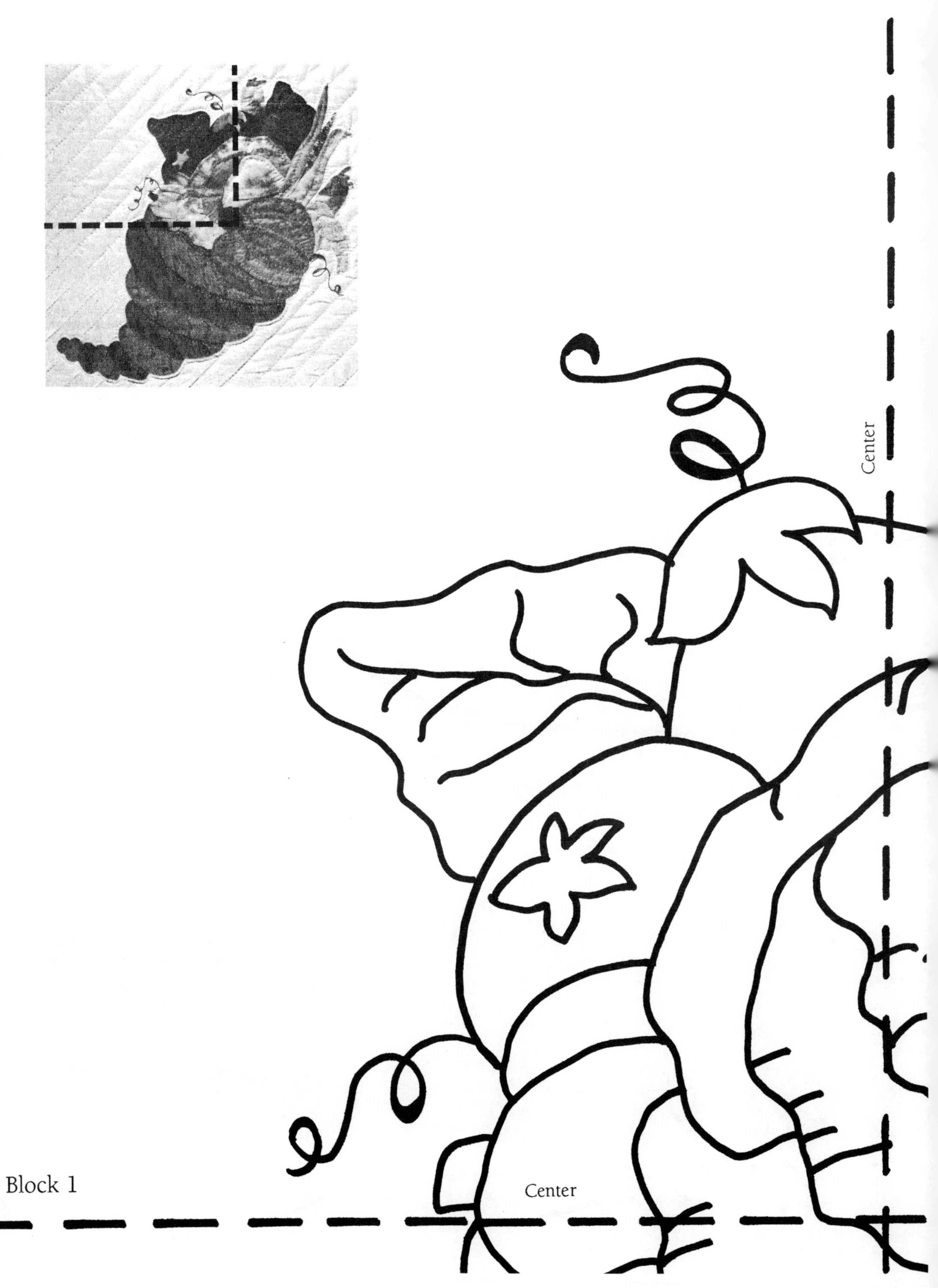
Center
Block 1
Center

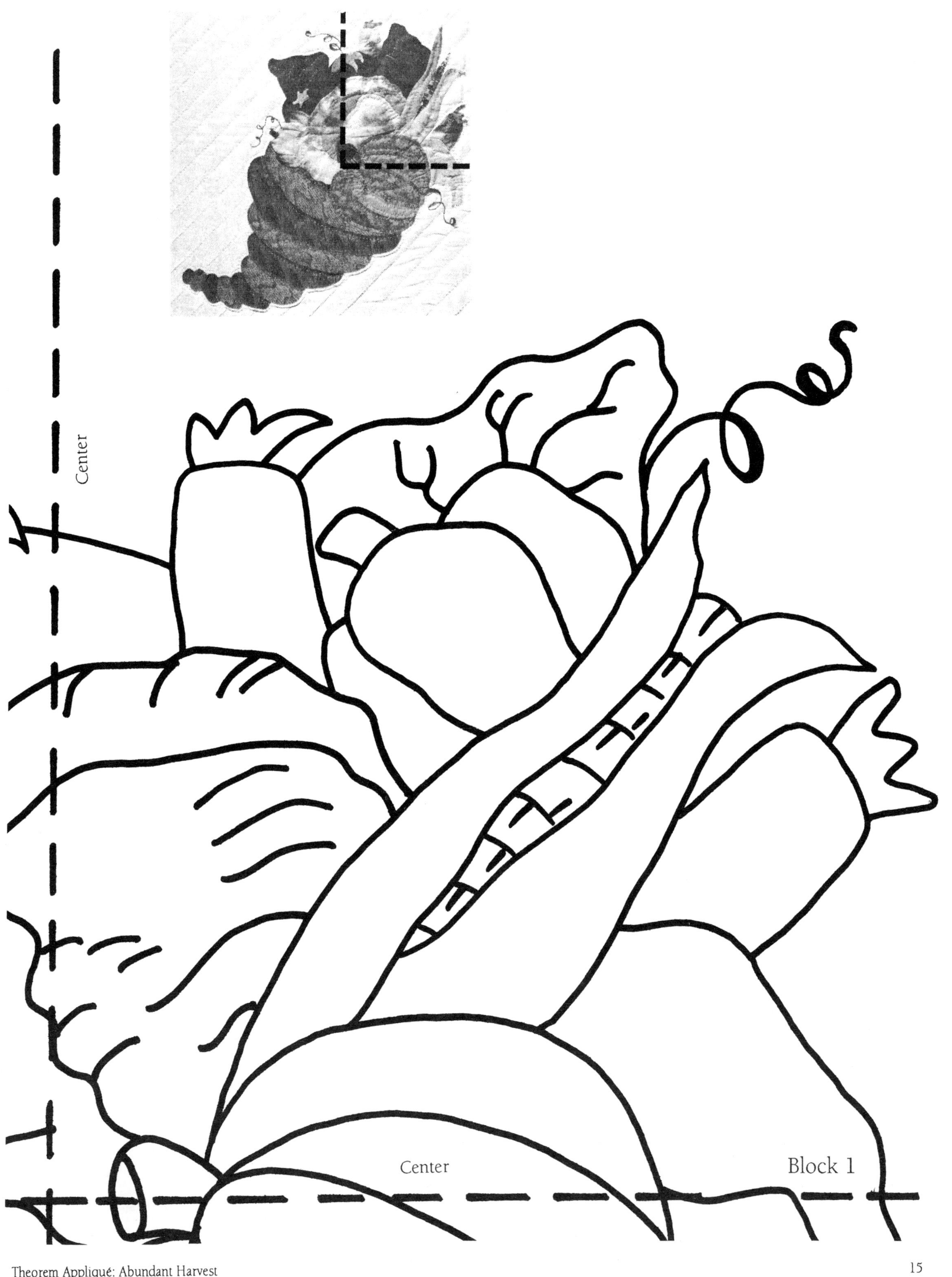
Center
Center
Block 1

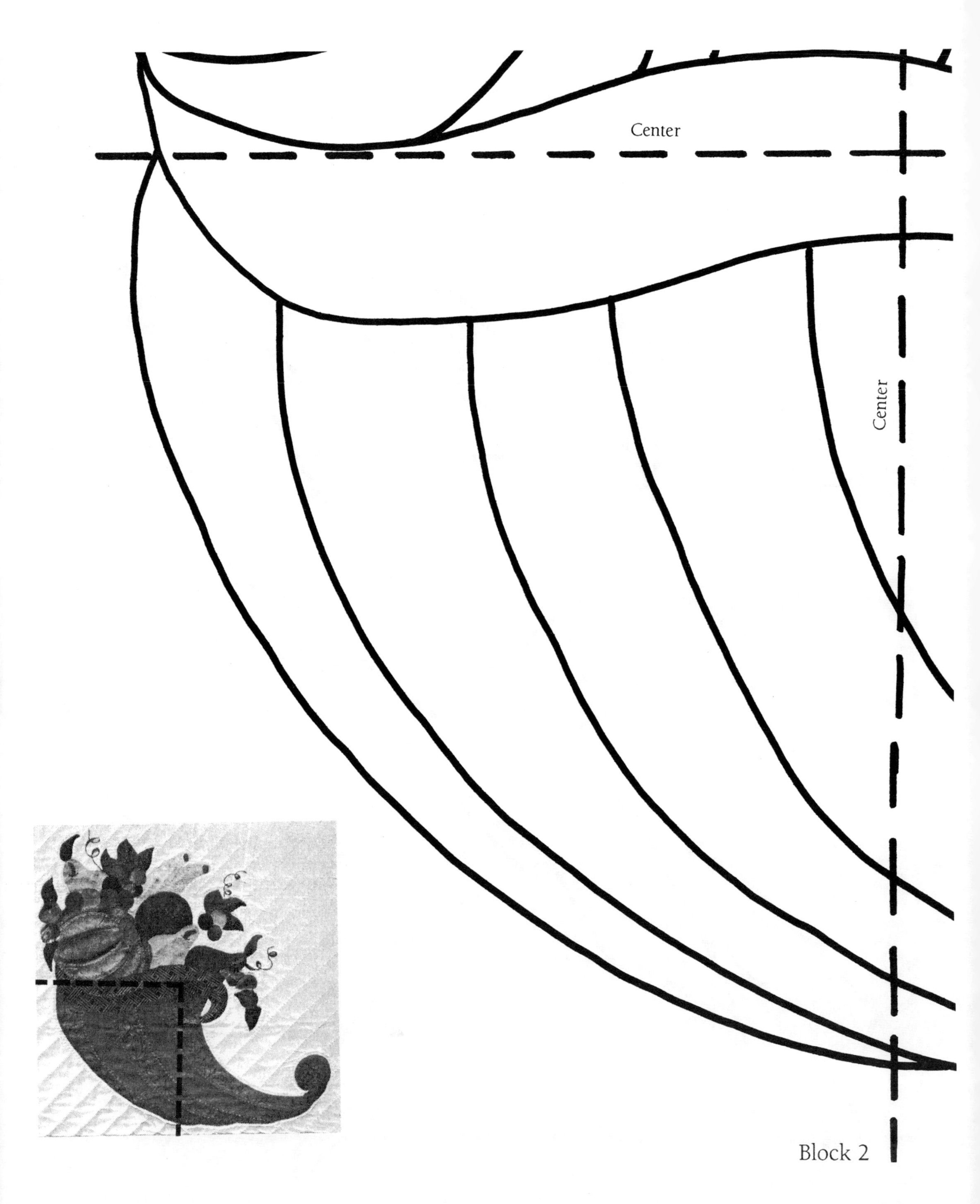

Block 2

Center
Center
Block 2

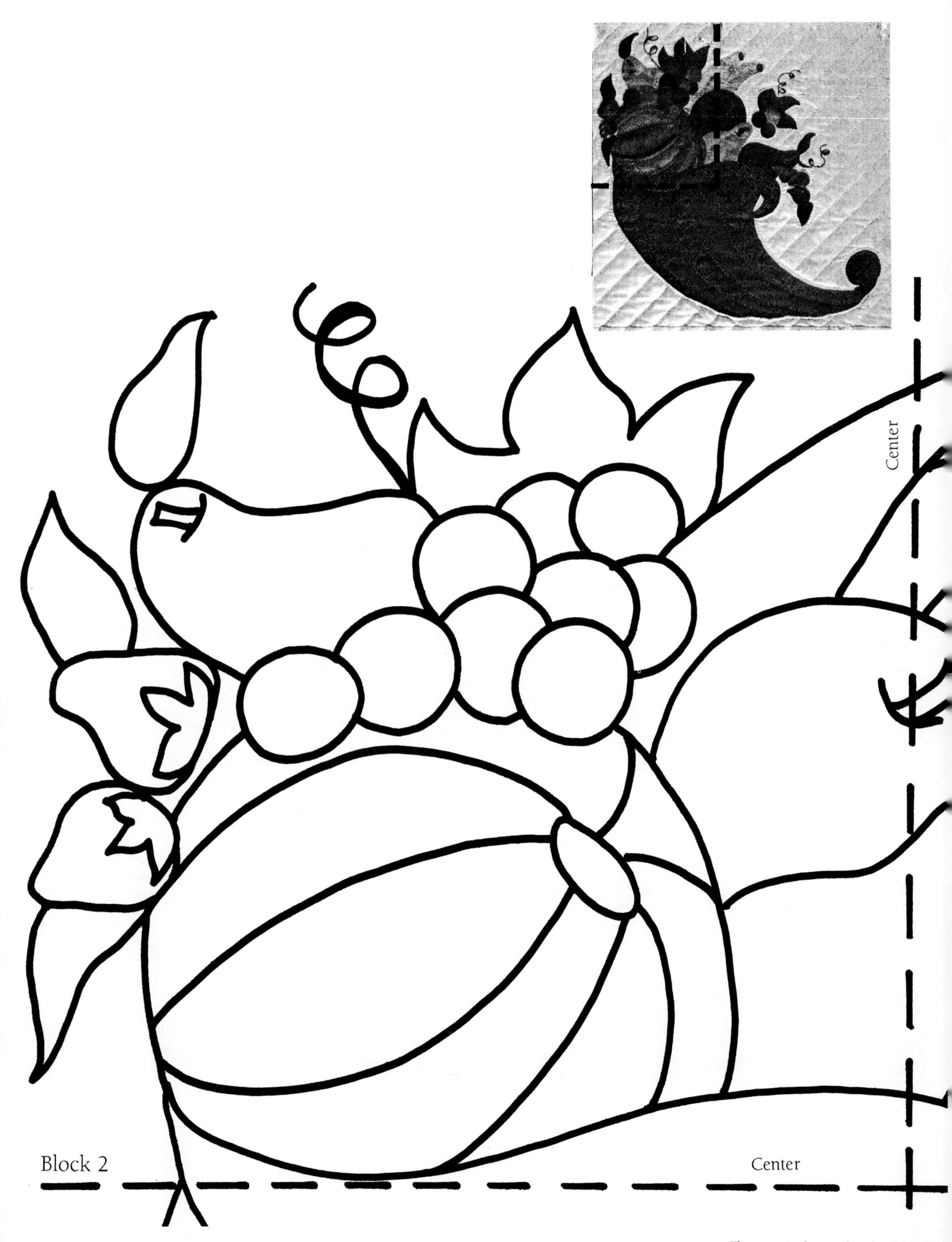
Center
Block 2
Center

Center
Center
Block 2

Center
Center
Block 3

Center
Center
Block 3

Center
Center
Block 3

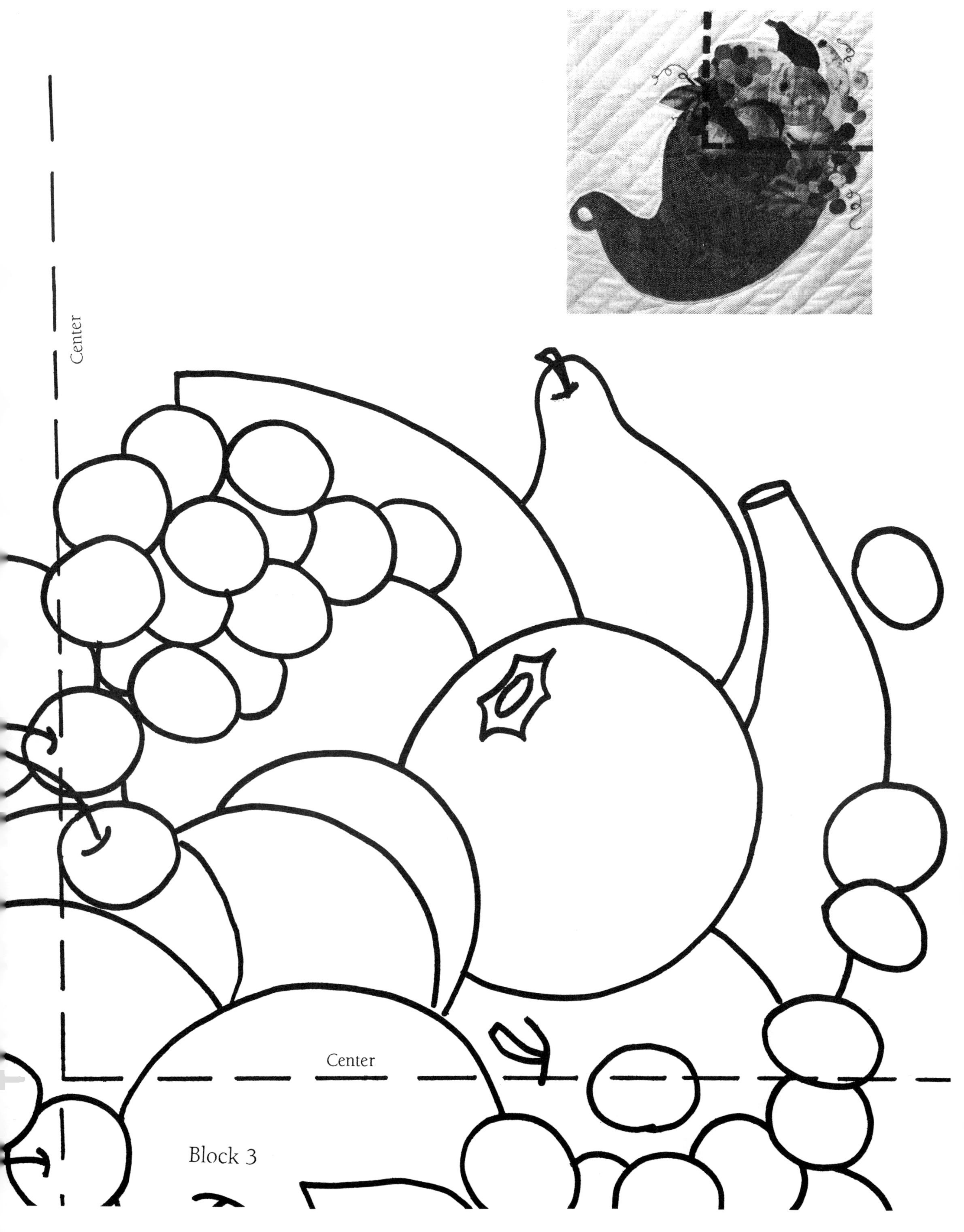
Center
Center
Block 3

Center
Center
Block 4

Center
Center
Block 4

Center
Center
Block 4

Center
Center
Block 4

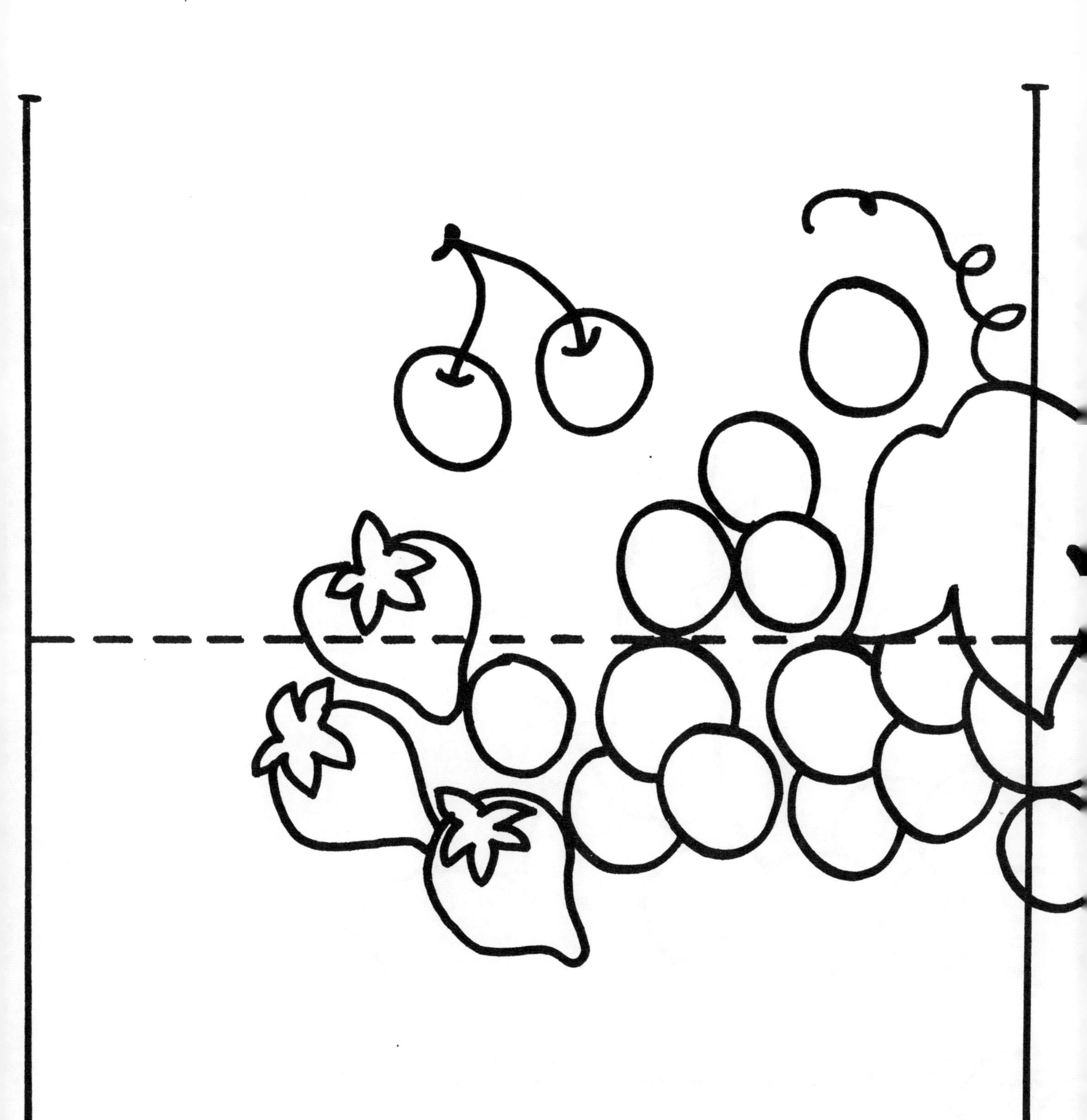

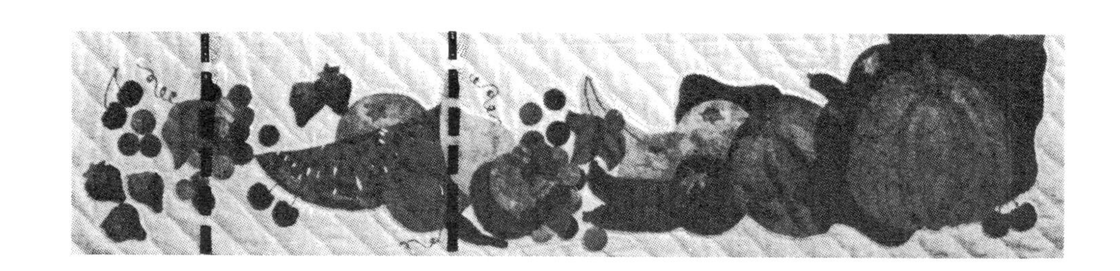

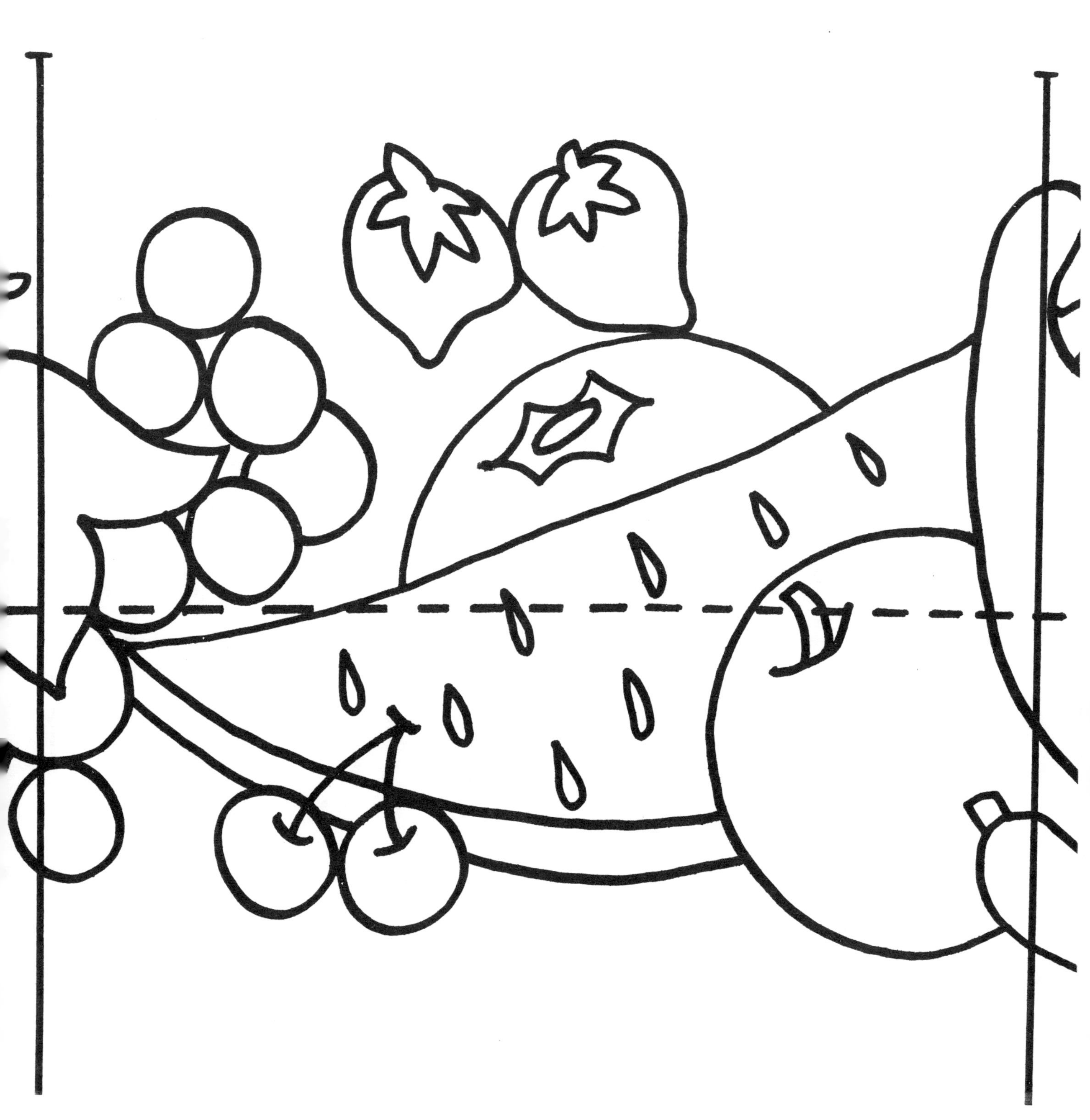

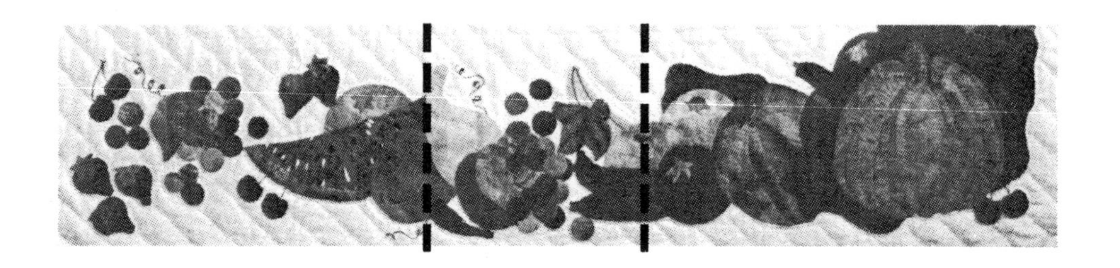

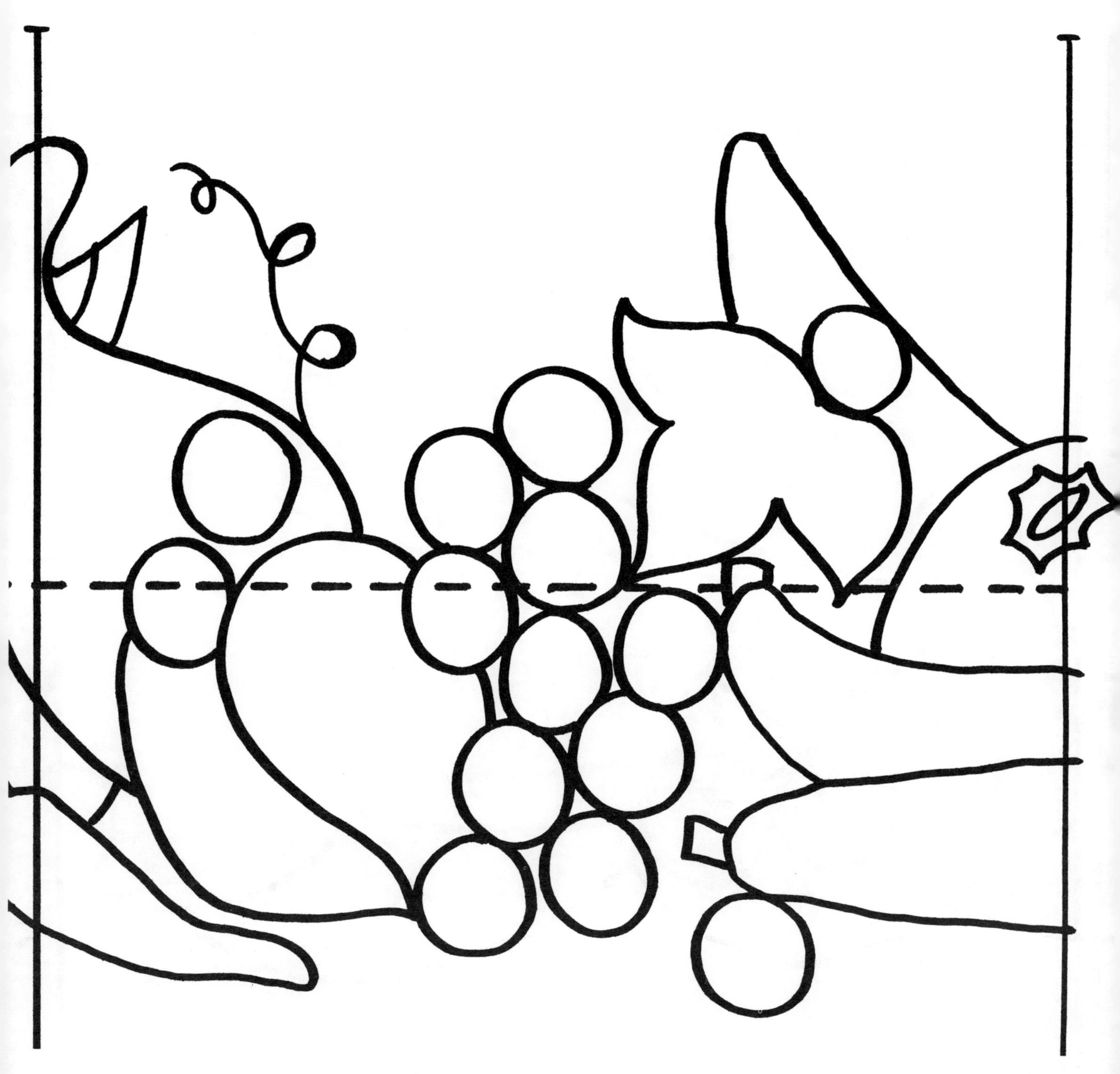

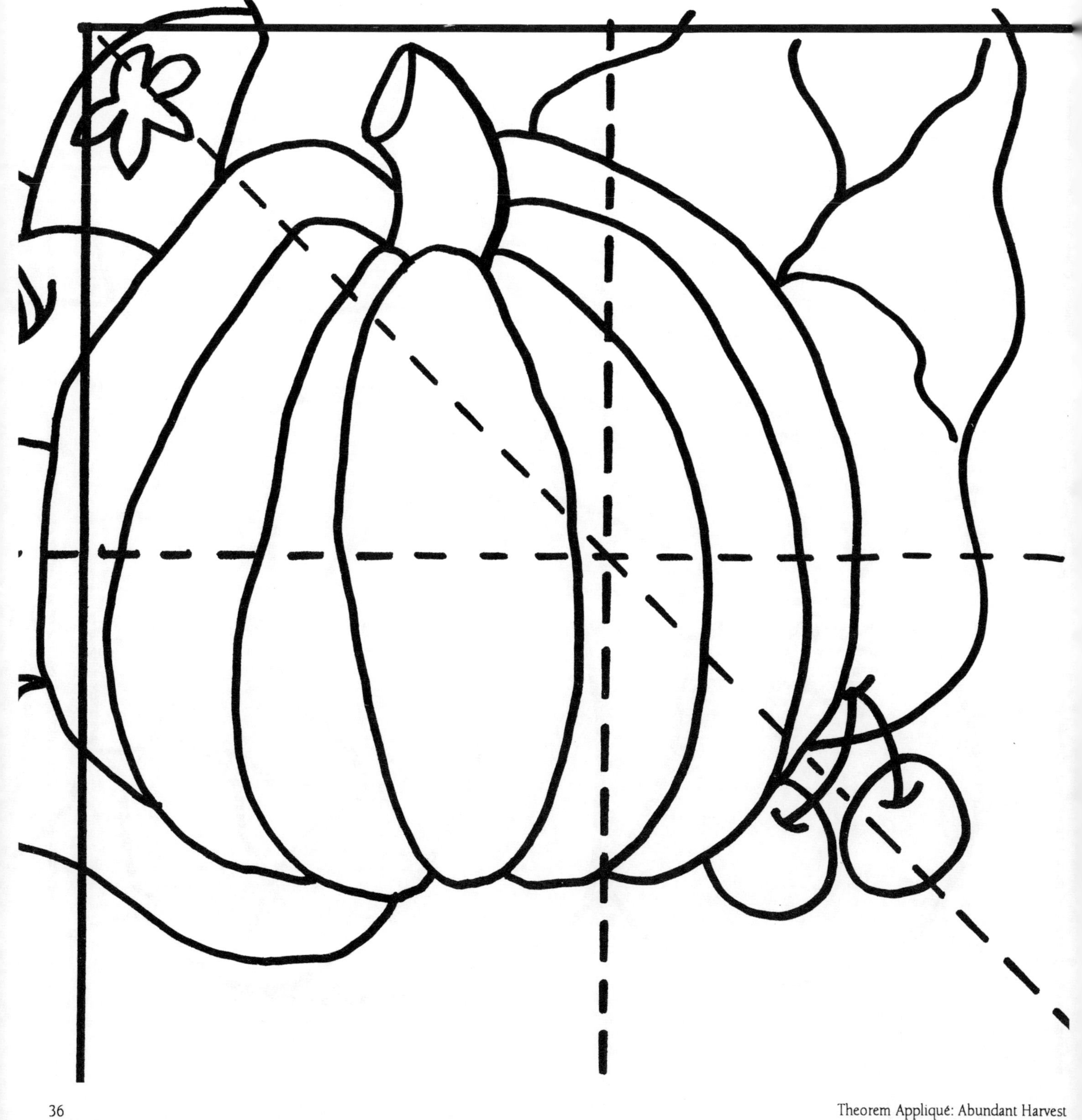

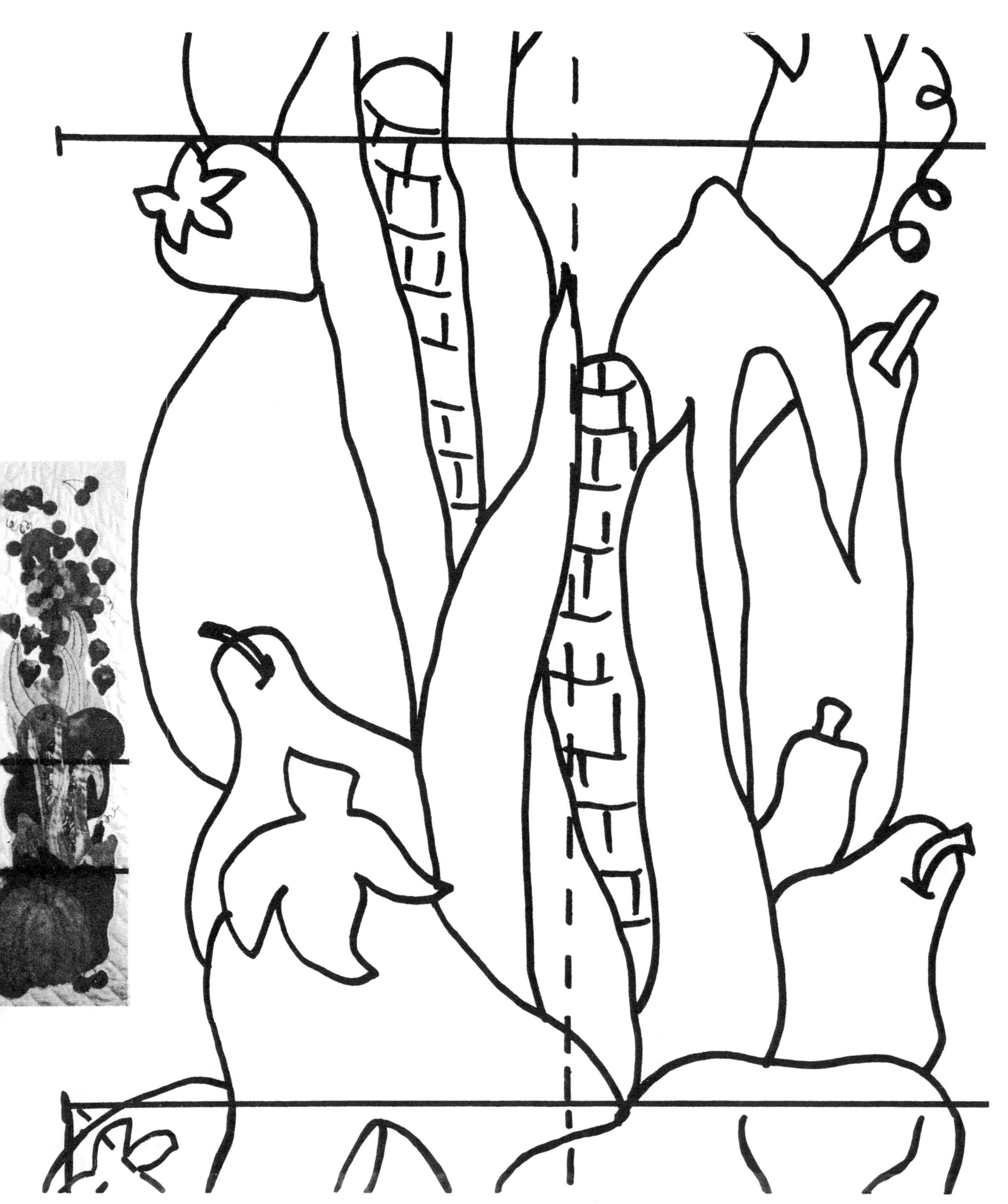

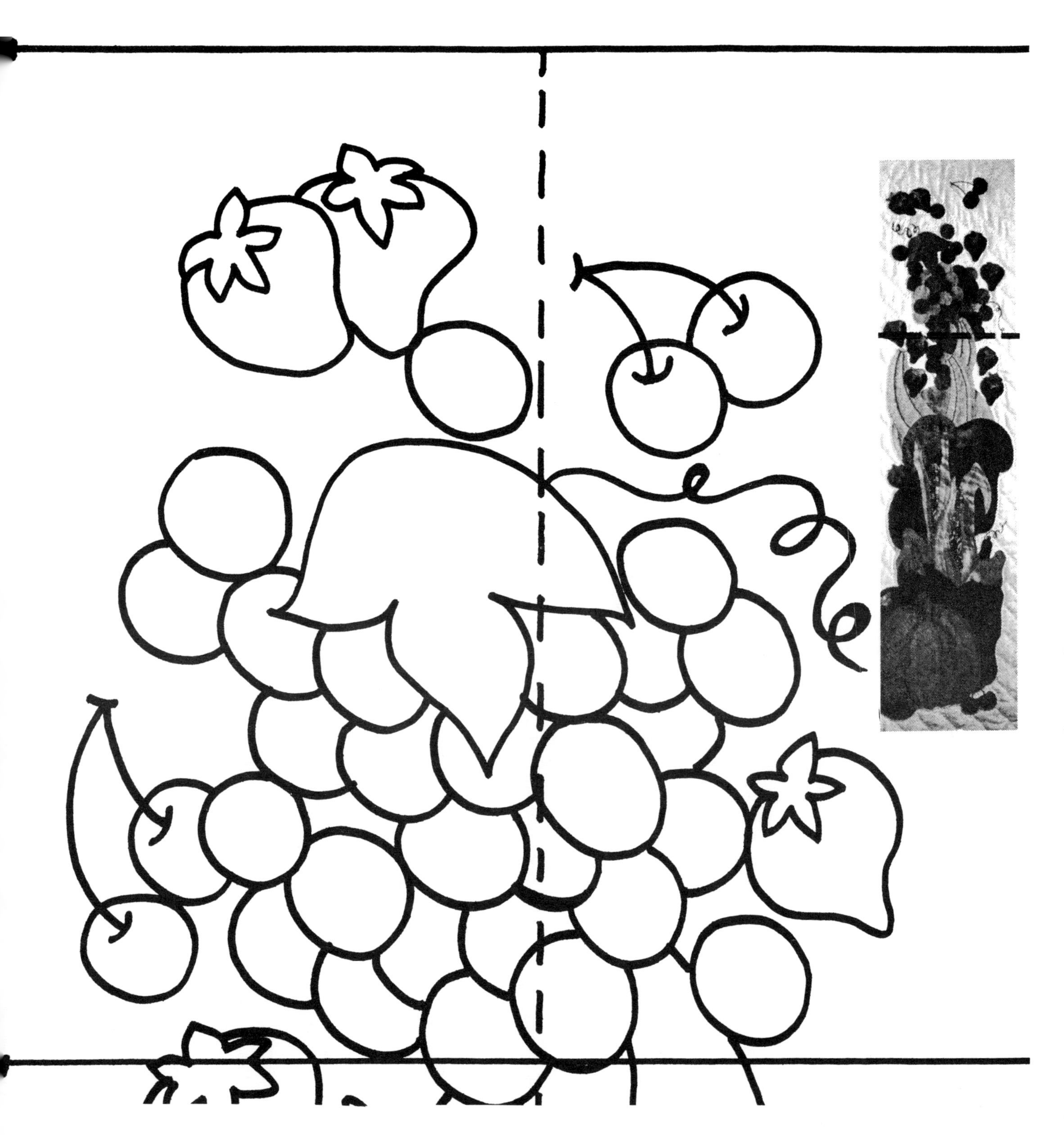

ALSO BY CHITRA PUBLICATIONS

MAGAZINES

Miniature Quilts • *Quilting Today* • *Traditional Quiltworks*

For subscription information, write to Chitra Publications, 2 Public Avenue, Montrose, PA 18801, or call 1-800-628-8244 (M-F, 8-4:30 EST)

BOOKS

The Best of Miniature Quilts, Volume 1 compiled by Patti Lilik Bachelder

Designing New Traditions in Quilts by Sharyn Squier Craig

Drafting Plus: 5 Simple Steps to Pattern Drafting and More! by Sharyn Squier Craig

Quilting Design Treasury by Anne Szalavary

Small Folk Quilters by Ingrid Rogler

A Stitcher's Christmas Album by Patti Lilik Bachelder

Tiny Amish Traditions by Sylvia Trygg Voudrie

Tiny Traditions by Sylvia Trygg Voudrie